OCTOBER MONTHLY ACTIVITIES

Written by Mary Ellen Sterling and Susan Schumann Nowlin

Illustrated by: Paula Spence, Keith Vasconcelles and Theresa Wright

Teacher Created Materials, Inc.
P.O. Box 1040
Huntington Beach, CA 92647
©1989 Teacher Created Materials, Inc.
Made in U.S.A.

ISBN 1-55734-152-4

Table of Contents

Table of Contents
(cont.)

INTRODUCTION

October Monthly Activities provides 80 dynamic pages of ready-to-use resources, ideas and activities that students love! All are centered around the themes, special dates and holidays of the month.

A complete "month-in-a-book," it includes:

- *A Calendar of Events* - ready to teach from and filled with fascinating information about monthly events, PLUS lots of fun ways you can apply these useful facts in your classroom.

- *A Whole Language Integrated Teaching Unit* - theme-based planning strategies, projects, lessons, activities, and more that provide a practical, yet imaginative approach to a favorite seasonal topic.

- *People, Places and Events* - an exciting series of activities that relate to the daily events in the Calendar of Events, and provide an innovative way for students to reinforce skills.

- *Management Pages* - a supply of reproducible pages that take you through the month, providing a wealth of valuable organizational aids that are right at your fingertips.

- *A Bulletin Board* - featuring a "hands-on" approach to learning; complete with full-size patterns, step-by-step directions, and tips for additional ways you can use the board.

Ideas and activities are also included for:

- *math*
- *art projects*
- *reading*
- *science*

- *geography*
- *social studies*
- *stationery*
- *creative writing*

- *literature ideas*
- *cooking*
- *reports*
- *seasonal words*

October Monthly Activities is the most complete seasonal book you'll ever find, and its convenient, reproducible pages will turn each month into a special teaching—and learning—experience!

USING THE PAGES

October Monthly Activities brings you a wealth of easy-to-use, fun-filled activities and ideas that will help you make the most of October's special themes and events. Although most of the activities are designed to be used within this month, if the holidays and traditions vary in your location, you may easily adapt the pages to fit your needs. Here are some tips for getting the most from your pages:

CALENDAR OF EVENTS

Each day makes note of a different holiday, tells about a famous person or presents a historical event. A question relating to each topic is provided (answers are on page 76). Teachers can use these facts in any number of ways including:

- *Post a copy of the calendar on a special bulletin board. Each day assign a different student to find the answer to that day's question. Set aside some time during the day to discuss the question with the whole class.*

- *Write the daily fact on the chalkboard. Have students keep a handwriting journal and copy the fact first thing each morning. They must use their best handwriting, of course!*

- *Use a daily event, holiday or famous person as a springboard for a Whole Language theme. Brainstorm with the class to find out what they already know about the topic. Explore the topic through literature, the arts, language and music.*

- *Older students can write a report on any of the daily topics. Younger students can be directed to draw a picture of the historical event or figure.*

- *Have students make up their own questions to go along with the day's event!*

- *Assign each student a different day of the calendar. Have them present a short oral report to the class on that day's topic.*

- *Use the daily events for math reinforcement. Ask how many: Days, weeks, months and years since the event occurred (for a real brain teaser, have students compute hours, minutes and seconds).*

- *Use in conjunction with the People, Places and Events section (pages 32 - 46).*

BLANK CALENDAR

Copy a calendar for each student. Have students use them to:

- *Write in daily assignments; check off each one as completed.*

- *Set daily goals—behavioral or academic.*

- *Copy homework assignments.*

- *Fill in with special dates, holidays, classroom or school events.*

- *Keep track of classroom chores.*

- *Use as a daily journal of feelings.*

- *Make ongoing lists of words to learn to spell.*

- *Answer the Question of the Day (see Calendar of Events).*

- *Record daily awards (stamps, stickers, etc.) for behavior or academic achievement.*

- *At the end of the day, evaluate their attitude, behavior, class work, etc. and give them a grade and explanation for the grade.*

- *Log reading time and number of pages read for free reading time.*

- *If there are learning centers in the classroom, let students keep track of work they have completed at each one or copy a schedule of times and days they may use the centers.*

- *Each day, write at least one new thing they learned.*

MANAGEMENT PAGES

Nifty ideas for extending the use of these pages.

- **Contracts** — *Help students set long or short term goals such as keeping a clean desk, reading extra books or improving behavior.*

- **Awards** — *Show students you appreciate them by giving awards for good attitude, helping, being considerate or for scholastic achievement. Students can give them to each other, their teacher or the principal!*

- **Invitations** — *Invite parents, grandparents, friends or another class to a classroom, school or sports event.*

- **Field Trip** — *Use for class trips or have students use in planning their own field trip to another country or planet.*

- **Supplies** — *Tell parents when you need art, craft, classroom, physical education or any other kind of supplies.*

- **Record Form** — *Place names in alphabetical order to keep track of classroom chores, completed assignments, contracts or permission slips.*

- **Stationery** — *Use as a creative writing pattern, for correspondence with parents, or for homework assignments.*

- **News** — *Fill in with upcoming weekly events and send home on Monday or let students fill in each day and take home on Friday. Younger students may draw a picture of something special they did or learned.*

- **Clip Art** — *Decorate worksheets, make your own stationery or answer pages. Enlarge and use for bulletin boards.*

> Hot Tips!

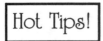 Be sure to look for the hot tips at the beginning of each section—they provide quick, easy and fun ways of extending the activities!

October Highlights

- Calendar of Events
- Spelling Activities
- Story Starters
- Gameboard
- Poetry
- Art Project
- And More!

Hot Tips!

Make a time line of events from the *October Calendar of Events*. Tape 8 1/2 x 11 inch sheets of construction paper in a row along the walls of the room (go around the corners, too!). Write one event per sheet of paper.

To stimulate creative writing, read Halloween poems, tales, and stories to the class. Turn off the lights in the room and have everyone sit in a circle. Have children tell their own funny or spooky stories or scary adventures.

OCTOBER

October is the tenth month of the year and has 31 days. On the Roman calendar, October was the eighth month. The name October comes from the Latin word for eight - octo.

Flower: Marigold   Birthstone: Opal

National Day (Nigeria)

1

On which continent is Nigeria located?

American inventor George Westinghouse was born in 1846.

6

What was his most famous invention?

Hoosier poet James Whitcomb Riley was born on this day in 1849.

7

What is a Hoosier?

Born in 1890, Eddie Rickenbacker was an American aviator in World War I.

8

What is an aviator?

Leif Ericson Day

9

What is a navigator?

The U.S. Navy was established in 1775.

13

What is the name of the 1st nuclear submarine?

William Penn, founder of Pennsylvania, was born in 1644.

14

What is Pennsylvania's nickname?

Poetry Day

15

What is your favorite poem?

Today is the 274th day of the year.

20

How many days remain in the year?

Birth date of Alfred Nobel, 1883.

21

What prize is named after him?

Rainmaking Day (African festival)

22

What is a cumulus cloud?

Canning Day

French chef Nicholas Appert developed a method of canning food in 1809.

23

What are some foods that come in cans?

Theodore Roosevelt, 26th President of the U.S., was born in 1858.

27

What popular children's toy is named after him?

Potetserie Day

In Norway, school children help harvest the potatoes.

28

How do you like potatoes prepared?

Turkey celebrates its national independence.

29

What two symbols are on the national flag of Turkey?

Birth date of Mohandas Gandhi in 1869. **2** *In which country did Gandhi live?*	American physician William C. Gorgas helped wipe out yellow fever during construction of the Panama Canal. **3** *What insect carries yellow fever and malaria?*	The 1st successful human-made satellite was launched by the Soviet Union in 1957. **4** *What is the name given to this satellite?*	Birthdate of Robert Goddard in 1882. "Father of Modern Rocketry" **5** *What is the name of the rocket that carried the first astronauts to the moon?*
Born in 1731, English scientist Henry Cavendish showed that water is composed of hydrogen and oxygen. **10** *How many glasses of water do you drink every day?*	First Lady Eleanor Roosevelt was born in 1884. **11** *What is a humanitarian?*		Columbus Day **12** *From which country did Columbus sail?*
Birth date of Noah Webster 1758. **16** *What is a dictionary?*	Black Poetry Day **17** *Who is Jupiter Hammon?*	Alaska Day Festival **18** *What is a kayak?*	Yorktown Day Marks the end of the Revolutionary War in 1781. **19** *What is a musket?*
	International Forgiveness Day **24** *What is one thing for which you would forgive your best friend? Forgive him or her today!*	John Strauss, Jr. ("Waltz King") was born in 1825. **25** *What is a waltz?*	The first motion picture with sound was shown on this date in 1927. **26** *What was the name of this film?*
Birthdate of John Adams, the second U.S. President. **30** *Who was the first U.S. President?*		Halloween **31** *What are 3 safety tips (or more!) for having a safe and happy Halloween?*	Other holidays celebrated this month are: ■ *Fire Prevention Week* ■ *Diwali (Festival of Lights, India)* ■ *Thanksgiving Day - Canada* ■ *United Nations Day* ■ *Nevada admitted to the union in 1864*

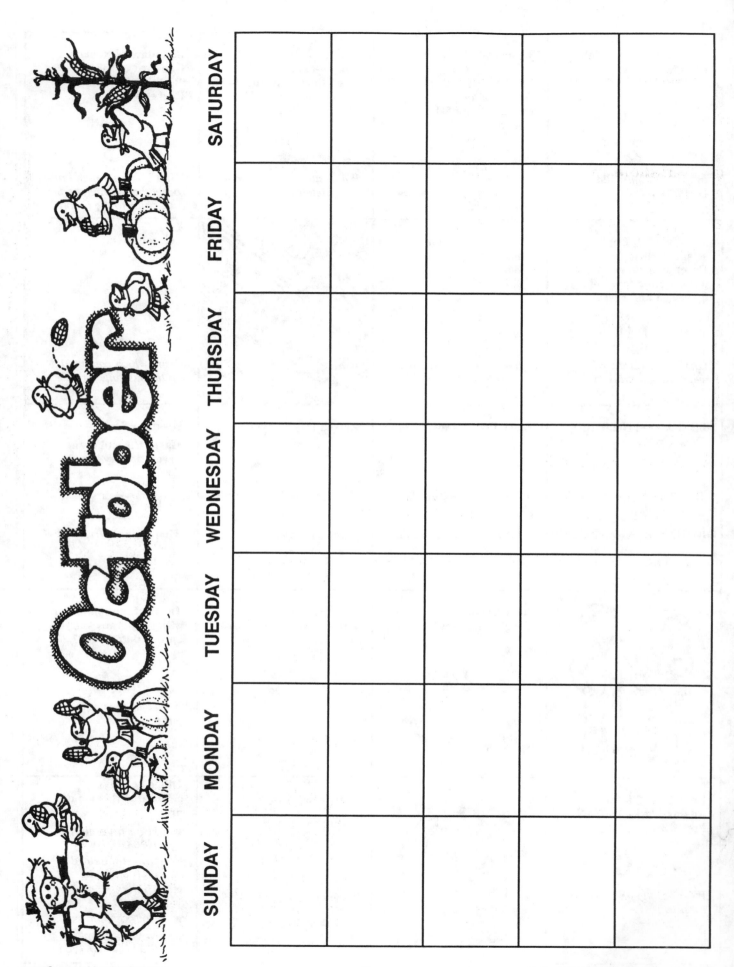

SUNDAY | MONDAY | TUESDAY | WEDNESDAY | THURSDAY | FRIDAY | SATURDAY

October Words and Activities

October Word Bank

pumpkin	apples	alarm	America
Halloween	costume	burn	broomstick
jack-o-lantern	ghost	Columbus	autumn
trick or treat	skeleton	flagship	candy
cider	black	October	owl
bobbing	orange	Niña	hoot
flashlight	voyage	Pinta	spider
house	fire	Santa Maria	Spain
carve	prevent	explorer	discover
spooky	smoke	New World	mask

Spelling Activities

Use the Word Bank above and give the students a choice of assignments below or have them try one of the following ideas in place of the standard spelling lessons.

- *Use an alphabet stencil to stencil any five words.*

- *Write six words using pumpkin seeds*

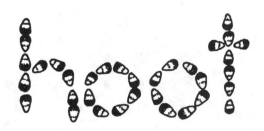

or candy corn. Glue the seeds or candy corn to tagboard or a piece of heavy cardboard.

- *Choose any eight words. Draw pictures of them.*

- *Write twelve words in order from shortest to longest.*

- *Write ten words in black and orange crayons! Use black for the consonants and orange for the vowels.*

- *Write a dozen words in chalk on black construction paper.*

October Story Starters

☐ Here's an enjoyable cooperative learning activity to use with your class. Pair the students and give each pair a paper bag, one orange and one black crayon. Have them write "trick or treat" across the top of the bag. Using only the letters contained in the phrase "trick or treat," they are to make as many words containing three or more letters as they can on the bag. Time them, and at the end of ten minutes the pair with the most correctly spelled words wins! (A reward could also be given to **all** groups who find twenty-five words.)

☐ Use unusual or humorous titles to stimulate creative writing. Brainstorm words, ideas, and phrases that might be used in a story with that title. Write all ideas on the chalkboard or on a flow chart for students to choose ideas. Group students to work on one story and an accompanying mural or illustration.

- Mr. Goblin's First Halloween
- The Right Way to Make Bat Wing Stew
- How the Raccoon Got His Mask
- Hoot Owl Meets the Black Cat
- The Apple Bobbing Contest
- Runaway Pumpkin

☐ Instead of story beginnings or story titles, give the students one of these story endings! They must write a beginning and middle to go with the ending.

- Little Owl was so glad to be back in her nest. She vowed never again to do anything that foolish.

- Finally, all the leaves were in a pile. Now he and Joe could run and jump into the center safely.

- Perky Pumpkin shook his head. "If only I'd known that two days ago, I never would have run away," he said remorsefully.

Name _____ **Date** _____

October Fractions

Color the pictures to make the fractions.

3/4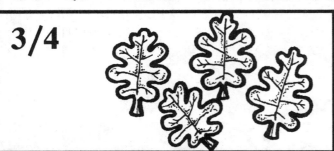

6/6

1/2

4/5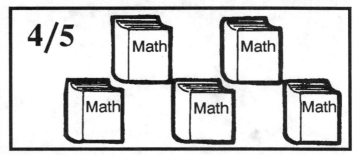

2/3

2/4

7/10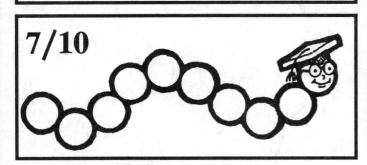

5/7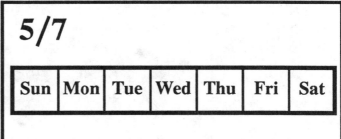

Challenge: Draw a picture for the fraction below. Color the correct amount to show the fraction.

5/8

October Worksheet

Directions _____

October Crossword

Fill in the crossword puzzle with words from the Word Bank.

Across

2. Columbus was a famous _____ .
4. October is _____ Prevention Week.
5. A fire has flames and _____ .
8. A Halloween color.
9. An arachnid.

Down

1. To stop something from happening.
3. This is worn on Halloween.
4. The main ship in a fleet.
6. The tenth month of the year.
7. A treat to eat.

WORD BANK

burn	spider	fire
candy	prevent	flagship
costume	orange	smoke
explorer	October	discover

Pumpkin Patch Gameboard

Directions:

Use this generic gameboard for any subject area. Label each pumpkin with a different math fact, science term, prefix, etc. (For more ideas see pages 78-80.) Each player will need a marker. Players can move one space at a time or determine the number of spaces moved with a die.

16

October Game Page

Stump the Class—An Indoor Game

If your students enjoy pantomimes, this version should be a real hit with them!

First, prepare a number of cards with one word circled at the top and a rhyming word written below it, e.g.

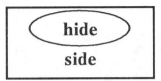

Then choose a student to take a word card and pantomime the circled word for the rest of the class. Once the word has been guessed, the class gets three more chances to guess the rhyming word that is written below the circled word on the card (the player does not pantomime this rhyming word). If the class does not guess the rhyming word within three guesses, the player has stumped the class and should be given a reward certificate or a special treat. Everyone will be eager to take his turn at this game!

Note:

To keep this activity from becoming too unruly, the student who is doing the pantomime should call on only those students who quietly raise their hand to make a guess.

Mouse's Tail—An Outdoor Game

Play this cooperative learning game in a large, open area. Divide the class into groups of six or eight. Have each group line up one behind the other, putting their arms on the shoulders of the person in front of them. The last person in each line tucks a handkerchief into his back pocket or in the back of his belt so that part of the handkerchief is showing.

At the signal, each mouse begins to chase its own "tail." The object is for the person at the head of the line to snatch the handkerchief from the last person in line. When the head finally captures the tail, they trade places: The head puts the handkerchief in his pocket to become the tail while the tail now becomes the head. And the chase is on again!

Poetry Page

- Celebrate World Poetry Day (October 15) by writing a class poem. One easy form to use is the couplet or two-line rhyming poem. Provide the first sentence for the class. Then brainstorm words that rhyme with the last word in the line. Together, the class can create a second line. After a little practice, pair the students to write and illustrate their own poems.

**There once was a ghost
Who sat on a post.**

- Another poetry form that will ensure student success is the cinquain. A cinquain is composed of five lines and each line does something different. Begin the writing process by working together with the class and brainstorming ideas. Then, as a class, compose a poem. Afterwards, student pairs or small groups can work together to write and illustrate their own cinquains.

Here is the outline for a cinquain.

1. title (use one word)
2. describe the title (use two words)
3. describe an action (use three words)
4. describe a feeling (use four words)
5. refer back to title (use one word)

**Pumpkin
Funny face
Looks and grins
Happily spying for goblins
Jack-o-lantern**

A Tricky Treat Bag

Materials:

Scissors; glue; crayons or markers; magazines; candy wrappers (optional); ribbon or yarn; hole punch and hole reinforcers or stapler; paper bag.

Directions:

Cut out pictures of candy and other treats and paste onto the front of the paper bag. (You may also use candy wrappers.) With crayons or markers write the words "Trick or Treat" at the top of the bag. Staple ribbon or yarn to the top of each side of the paper bag for a handle or punch a hole on either side of the bag. Put a reinforcer around both sides of each hole. String yarn or ribbon through the holes.

Pet Trick Or Treat Bag

If your pet could go trick-or-treating, what would he collect? Draw or cut out pictures from books and magazines to put on the paper bag shape.

Don't have a pet? Make one up or adopt a dinosaur for a pet.

October Whole Language Unit:

PUMPKINS

- How to Write a Unit
- Lessons
- Worksheets
- And More!

Encourage curiosity about pumpkins by setting up a display of pumpkins of various sizes and shapes. Set out paints or colored markers; have students paint or draw faces on the pumpkins.

Group students according to colors! Everyone wearing something green is in one group, everyone wearing something white is in another group. If a group is too large, break it down further by articles of clothing - belts, hats, sneakers, etc.

20

How to Plan

Because of their bright color and unusual size and shape, pumpkins are appealing and intriguing to youngsters. Then, too, pumpkins undergo an almost magical transformation when they are carved into jack-o-lanterns. A study unit based on pumpkins provides numerous opportunities for learning. Begin your unit by following these step-by-step guidelines.

 Set the mood in your classroom with a "pumpkin" bulletin board. Pages 69 to 75 contain all the patterns you'll need to create a *Pumpkin Patch* (see diagram below). Pumpkins should be left blank for now; they can be labeled after brainstorming with the students.

 Assemble your resources: Books, films, tapes, games, texts, and real objects.

 Plan general lessons integrating math, reading, art, music, language, and physical education.

 Outline your lesson goals and objectives.

 Make evaluation tools that are appropriate for the lesson.

 After the first week of pumpkin lessons, evaluate and then plan the next week.

Pumpkin Patch

Projects and Lessons

The following pages describe specific lessons and ideas that you can use to integrate the curriculum through the study of pumpkins.

- **Set up a display table** *with a number of pumpkins that vary in size and shape. Include some books on Halloween or a story or poem about jack-o-lanterns. Read the stories and poems aloud to the class.*

(See page 63)

- **Keep parents informed** *about upcoming activities. Compose a class letter to send home and let students copy the message on their own stationery (see diagram at left). Use the letter to enlist volunteers or request any necessary supplies you'll be needing throughout this unit.*

Language

- **Brainstorm with the students.** *Find out what they already know about pumpkins. Ask what else they would like to find out about pumpkins. List all appropriate responses on the chalkboard or a flip chart. Use these ideas to plan specific lessons. Hint: You may want to record vocabulary words on the pumpkins or leaves of the Pumpkin Patch bulletin board.*

Science and Math

- **Group the students** *(make sure that the mix includes some with stronger and some with weaker academic abilities). Buy five same-size pumpkins and give one to each group. As a group, have them weigh their pumpkin using a non-standard unit of measure. Each group should use a different standard and results could be compared on a class chart. (Older students can weigh their pumpkins using standard metric measurement. First have them estimate what the pumpkin weighs, then weigh the pumpkin.)*

	Group 1	Group 2	Group 3	Group 4
Number of units	2,875			
Unit of measurement	paper clips	pencils	blocks	_____

Projects and Lessons

Science and Math

- **After weighing the pumpkins, engage students in an estimation game.** *First, have each group estimate how many seeds are in their pumpkin; record all guesses on group charts. Then cut the pumpkin in half and count the seeds. To reinforce the concept of place value, supply each group with several paper plates. As students count the seeds, group sets of ten in each plate. After counting the actual number of seeds, record the results on the chart and compare with the estimates. (For more in-depth coverage of this activity see pages 36 and 37 in TCM229 Problem-Solving Science Investigations.)*

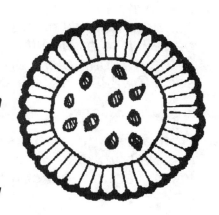

Language

- **Write pumpkin couplets.** *Practice as a class before grouping students to work on this writing project (see Poetry Page, page 18). Supply the first line for their poems (some samples are below) or have the children write their own. Write the poems on pumpkin shapes (see pattern on page 31).*

- Clever pumpkin, fat and cute...
- Six little pumpkins in a row...
- Pumpkins on a starry night...
- One lone pumpkin in a pumpkin patch...

Language and Art

- **Roast the pumpkin seeds.** *Spread pumpkin seeds on a cookie sheet. Bake at 350° until brown. Let the children eat the roasted pumpkin seeds. Brainstorm words that describe how the roasted seeds taste, look, feel, and smell. Record the words on a Sense Matrix (see page 50) or record the words on a Pumpkin Word Bank. (Enlarge the pumpkin pattern on page 31 and write the words on it.) These words can later be used in creative writing, social studies reports, or science investigations. Or, make a pumpkin mosaic. Glue dried seeds to a paper plate. Hang with yarn or ribbon.*

Science and Language

- **Make pumpkin bread.** *Mix the first four ingredients on page 25. Fold in remaining ingredients. Pour into greased 9 x 5 x 3 inch pan. Bake at 350° for 50 minutes or until done. Cool before cutting. As a follow-up, write the recipe on a pumpkin shape (see pattern on page 31).*

Projects and Lessons

Science

- **Present this hypothesis to the students:** *Will a pumpkin with a slit cut in it rot more quickly than an uncut pumpkin?* Use the **Science Experiment Form**, *page 51, to outline the steps. Have students keep a daily journal of changes in the two pumpkins and draw pictures of any changes. (For more information see TCM229, Problem-Solving Science Investigations.)*

Language and Science

- **Compare and contrast pumpkins with other fruits and vegetables.** *In large or small groups list ways they are alike and ways they are different. Prepare a Venn diagram that compares a pumpkin with one other food. See the sample below.*

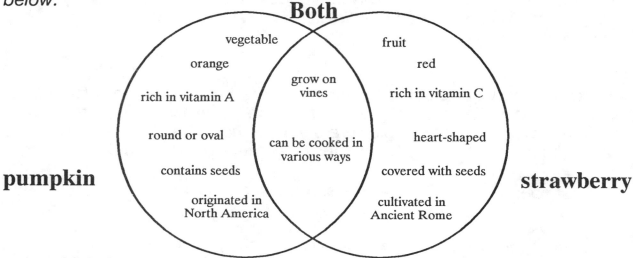

Both

pumpkin   **strawberry**

- vegetable
- orange
- rich in vitamin A
- round or oval
- contains seeds
- originated in North America

- grow on vines
- can be cooked in various ways

- fruit
- red
- rich in vitamin C
- heart-shaped
- covered with seeds
- cultivated in Ancient Rome

Language and Math

- **Supply a variety of pumpkin foods such as pie, soup, ice cream, bread, etc.** *(Enlist parent volunteers to donate these foods.) Before actual tasting begins, have the students predict which pumpkin food they will prefer. Prepare a graph of these preferences. After tasting the foods, compare predicted preferences to actual preferences.*

	PUMPKIN PREDICTIONS
Soup	John
Bread	Debbie
Pie	David
Ice Cream	Sue

Children can make their own marker to record their predictions.

Pumpkin Bread

All the ingredients for pumpkin bread are listed below. Next to each ingredient tell how much you would need if you **doubled** the recipe. In the far right column, write how much of each ingredient you would need if you were to cut the recipe in **half**. Some have been done for you.

Ingredients	Double		Half	
½ c. sugar	1	c.		c.
½ c. vegetable oil		c.		c.
1 c. pumpkin		c.		c.
2 eggs		eggs	1	egg
1 ½ c. flour		c.		c.
1 tsp. baking soda		tsp.		tsp.
1 tsp. baking powder	2	tsp.		tsp.
1 tsp. cinnamon		tsp.		tsp.
½ tsp. nutmeg		tsp.		tsp.
¼ tsp. salt		tsp.	⅛	tsp.
½ c. raisins		c.		c.
½ c. walnuts		c.		c.

Directions for making Pumpkin Bread can be found on page 23.

Challenge: Convert the cups and teaspoons above to metric measurement!

Math Facts Review

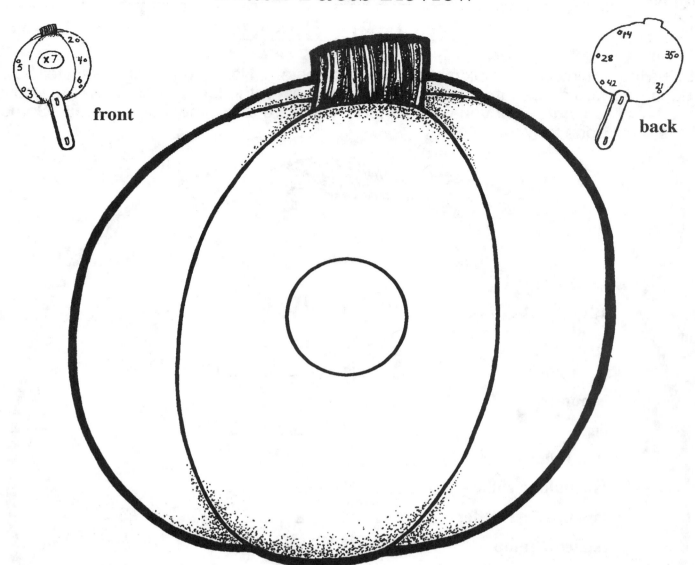

front

back

Directions: Make as many pumpkin shapes as you will need. Glue to heavy tagboard for durability; cut out. In the circle write an operation sign (see operation signs below) and the number you want to review (see diagram). Punch holes along the perimeter of the pumpkin. Write a different number next to each hole punched. Turn the pumpkin over and write the answers to the problems next to the proper hole. Laminate and cut out. Staple two craft sticks together to the bottom of each pumpkin placing one stick on each side of the pumpkin (see diagram).

To Play: One child faces the front of the pumpkin, while another child faces the back of the pumpkin. The child facing the front puts a pencil through a hole next to a number and says the problem aloud. (In the diagram, for example, seven will be multiplied by each number. If the child puts the pencil in the three, he would say, "Seven times three equals twenty-one.") The child facing the back of the pumpkin checks the answers. After all problems have been computed, the children trade places.

> ## Operation Signs: $+$, $-$, $\times$, $\div$

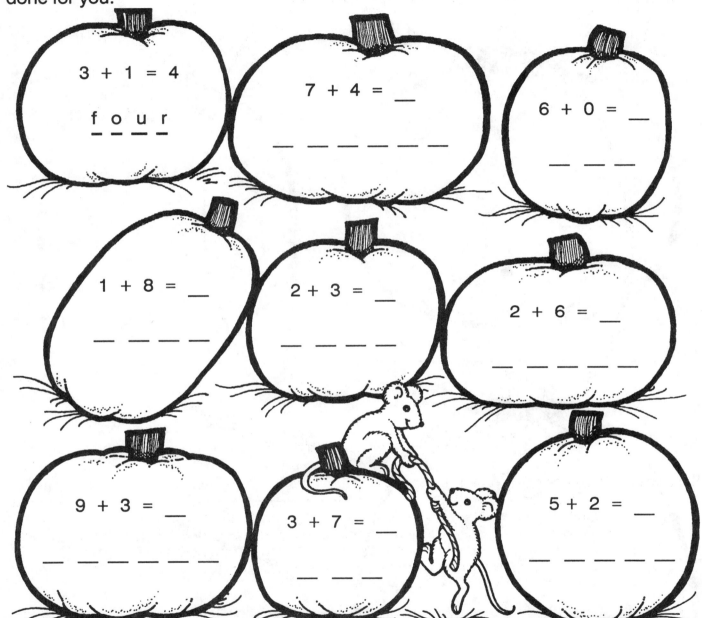

Name the Number

Find the sums. Then write the word name of each answer on the lines. One has been done for you.

3 + 1 = 4

f o u r

7 + 4 = __

____

6 + 0 = __

____

1 + 8 = __

____

2 + 3 = __

____

2 + 6 = __

____

9 + 3 = __

____

3 + 7 = __

____

5 + 2 = __

____

Can't remember how to spell a number name? Use this WORD BANK to help you.

seven	eight	nine
ten	six	twelve
five	eleven	four

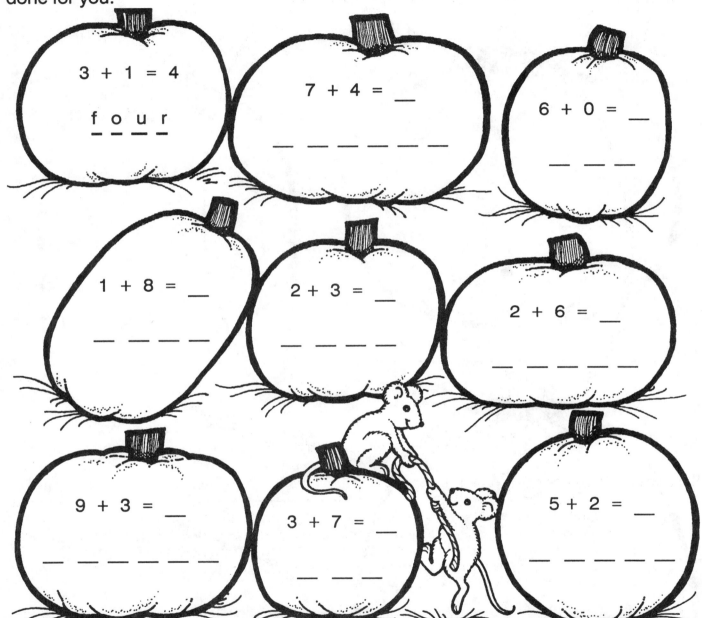

Make Your Own Faces!

Draw a different face on each pumpkin. Write a title or name for each one.

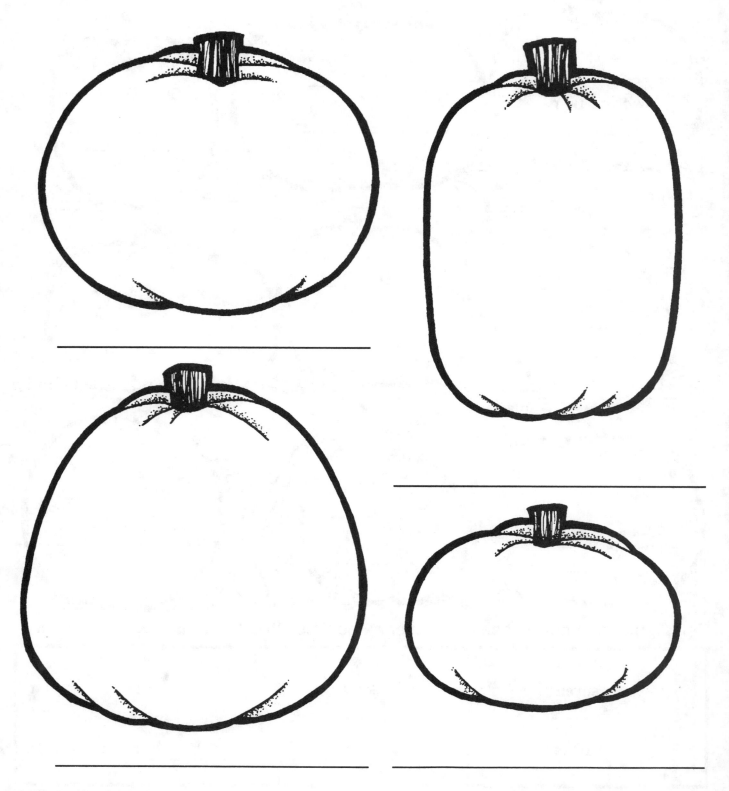

Up and Down Words

Find a partner to work with. You will need a pencil and a dictionary. Find and write a word that begins with the first letter in the first line and either contains or ends with the second letter in the line. For example, on the line P_____N you could write **picnic** or **pigeon**. Score one point for each letter in the word. Challenge another team to beat your total.

Points

P _____   N _____   ___

U _____   I _____   ___

M _____   K _____   ___

P _____   P _____   ___

K _____   M _____   ___

I _____   U _____   ___

N _____   P _____   ___

Total ___

On Your Own! Choose your own word to write up and down—down on the left and up on the right. Then write words across.

Points

_ _____   _ _____   ___

_ _____   _ _____   ___

_ _____   _ _____   ___

_ _____   _ _____   ___

_ _____   _ _____   ___

_ _____   _ _____   ___

_ _____   _ _____   ___

Total ___

Name _____ Date _____

How to Write a Report

Use the steps outlined in this linear spiral to help you write a report.

CHOOSE A TOPIC

Keep it specific. SPORTS is too general; BASEBALL is a specific sport.

WRITE FIVE QUESTIONS ABOUT THE TOPIC

1. How is it played?
2. How and where did it originate?
3. What equipment is used?
4. Who are some famous players?
5. What are some of the rules?

PUT THE QUESTIONS IN GOOD ORDER

2.
1.
5.
3.
4.

DO RESEARCH

Use a variety of books: Texts, biographies, encyclopedias, and other reference books. Write notes on index cards.

WRITE THE REPORT

Write four or five sentences about each of the five questions.

BIBLIOGRAPHY

At the end of your report write the title and author of all the books you researched.

YOUR TURN

- Choose a topic and write it on the line. _____

- Write five questions about the topic.

    1. _____
    2. _____
    3. _____
    4. _____
    5. _____

- Put the questions in good order.

    1st _____ 2nd _____ 3rd _____ 4th _____ 5th _____

- Now you are ready to do your research, write your report and bibliography.

Creative Writing Pattern

For suggested art and creative writing activities see page 23.

#152 October Monthly Activities

October People, Places, and Events

- Columbus Day
- Halloween Story
- Fire Prevention Checklist
- Canada's Thanksgiving Day
- And More!

The learning pages and ideas in this section are extensions of the people, places, and events from this month's calendar. They can be used to introduce a topic, reinforce or follow-up a lesson, or as independent projects. Many of these activities can easily be incorporated into your Whole Language Program; others are suitable for Cooperative Learning Projects.

Hot Tips!

If some of these work pages are too simple for your students, make the worksheets more challenging by covering the Word Bank before you make duplicates!

Wire baskets make great containers for finished work. Label one "In" for children to place their completed worksheets. Label another basket "Out" for work that has been graded and is ready to be returned to the students.

Name _____   **Date** _____

Columbus Day

(Columbus Day, October 12)

> *On October 12, 1492 Christopher Columbus discovered a new land. He had traveled from Palos, Spain on August 3, 1492 with a fleet of three small ships, the Niña, the Pinta, and the Santa Maria. King Ferdinand and Queen Isabella of Spain had given Columbus money for the journey because they wanted him to bring back spices and gold from the Indies. However, he did not land in the Indies. Instead, he had landed in the Bahamas off the coast of Cuba. Since Columbus thought he had sailed to the Indies, he called the natives Indians.*
>
> *The New World was full of things Columbus and his crew had never seen before such as corn, potatoes, cocoa beans, tobacco, and peanuts. Today, Columbus Day is celebrated in the U.S. on the second Monday of October. Many Latin American countries also celebrate this day in honor of their Spanish heritage.*

1. **Knowledge**

   How many ships were in Columbus' fleet? What were the names of the ships?

2. **Comprehension**

   Construct a pictorial time line showing the events of Columbus' voyage to the New World.

3. **Application**

   Draw a map of the route Columbus took from Spain to the New World. Be sure to label the countries.

4. **Analysis**

   If you were assigned to sail West to find a new land, what are the most important supplies you would bring with you?

5. **Synthesis**

   Write a diary account of the last five days of Columbus' voyage in which he found the New World. Imagine how the sailors might have felt after sailing for so long.

6. **Evaluation**

   The King and Queen of Spain wanted Christopher Columbus to bring back spices and gold from the Indies. Instead, he brought back items such as cocoa beans, potatoes, and tobacco. Do you think his discoveries were more valuable or less valuable than the gold and spices he was supposed to have brought back?

A Famous Explorer

(Columbus Day, October 12)

Write the first letter of each picture below to learn an important fact about a famous explorer.

___ ___ ___ ___ ___ ___ ___ ___

___ ___ ___ ___ ___ **the**

___ ___ ___   ___ ___ ___ ___ ___ ,

___ ___ ___ ___ ___ ___ ___ ___ ___ ___ , **on**

___ ___ ___ ___ ___ ___ ___ **12, 1492.**

Halloween Story

(Halloween, October 31)

Read the paragraph below. Fill in the blanks with words from the WORD BANK below.

① _____ 31 is a special ② _____ for children in the United

States and Canada. It is Halloween, a time when ③ _____ dress up as

monsters, ④ _____, animals, or other characters. They go from

house to house to collect ⑤ _____ and treats.

" ⑥ _____ !" is what they say. Sometimes ⑦ _____

are held in the evening. ⑧ _____ is a popular beverage,

and bobbing for ⑨ _____ is a ⑩ _____ that everyone can enjoy.

Trick or treat	**children**	**parties**
game	**October**	**cider**
candy	**ghosts**	**holiday**
Halloween	**apples**	**candle**

Holiday Creative Writing

Cut out the cards below and sort into three piles—Characters, Places, and Actions. Shuffle the cards and place face down in their respective piles. Have students choose one card from each pile and write a creative story using the ideas from all three cards. Pairs or small groups can work together on this project.

CHARACTERS **PLACES** **ACTIONS**

Halloween Fill-in

(Halloween, October 31)

Fill in the blanks below to make some Halloween words using words from the WORD BANK. Some clues are given to help you.

1. __ __ __ __ __ y

2. __ __ __ __ k

3. __ u __ __ __ __ __

4. __ __ a __ __ __

5. __ __ __ s __ __ __ __

6. __ r __ __ __ __ __

7. __ __ o __ __

8. __ __ __ e

9. __ p __ __ __ __

10. __ __ __ __ l __

WORD BANK

pumpkin	candy
black	costume
orange	spooky
mask	treat
ghost	apple

Silly Scarecrow

This brad project can be used in any number of ways. It can be an art project, a follow-up to a literature selection, a puppet for a puppet play, or a character for a bulletin board. No matter which one you choose, you can be sure that your students will be delighted with their own Silly Scarecrow.

Materials:

Crayons or colored markers; scissors; brads; white or colored construction paper.

Directions:

Duplicate all pattern pieces (pages 38 and 39) onto tagboard; draw a silly face on the scarecrow; color and cut out all pattern pieces; attach the same letter points with a brad (A to A, B to B, etc.); make your scarecrow do a silly dance; give him a silly name.

Hot Tip!

Make this art project easier for young children by duplicating pattern pieces onto colored paper. Direct children to color the scarecrow's hat and shoes only.

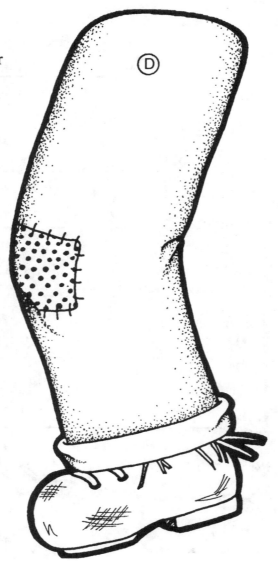

Silly Scarecrow

(cont.)

For complete directions on assembling this project, see page 38.

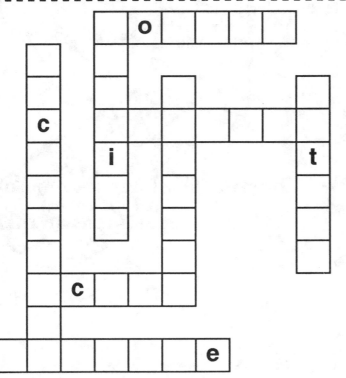

Name _____ **Date** _____

October Scrambler

Unscramble the letters next to each name below to find out their occupation. Use the WORD BANK to help you.

1. Eddie Rickenbacker   vatiora   __ __ __ __ __ __ __
2. James Whitcomb Riley   tope   __ __ __ __
3. Theodore Roosevelt   dnetsiper   __ __ __ __ __ __ __ __ __
4. Nicholas Appert   hecf   __ __ __ __
5. Henry Cavendish   tiscients   __ __ __ __ __ __ __ __ __
6. Johann Strauss, Jr.   rescmoop   __ __ __ __ __ __ __ __
7. Noah Webster   ertirw   __ __ __ __ __ __
8. George Westinghouse   troinenv   __ __ __ __ __ __ __ __

WORD BANK

chef   inventor   aviator   writer

composer   poet   scientist   president

Fill in the spaces with the names of some more occupations listed below. Some clues have been given to help you.

actor   rancher

dentist   artist

teacher   doctor

accountant   athlete

Name _____ Date _____

Fire Prevention Checklist

Fire Prevention Week is observed during the second week of October. Find out what you can do to prevent fires in your home by checking all items on the list below. Discuss each item with your family.

☐ I know the emergency number to call in case of fire.

☐ Our family has a planned fire escape route.

☐ Our family has a fire extinguisher; everyone in the family knows its location and how to use it.

☐ Pot handles are kept pointed away from the edge of the cooking surface.

☐ There are smoke detectors throughout the house.

☐ All electrical appliance cords are in good shape.

☐ The electrical outlets are not overloaded.

☐ The fireplace has a well-fitting screen.

☐ Foods are closely supervised while cooking.

☐ Oily rags are stored in tightly sealed metal containers.

☐ Papers, trash, and paints are kept away from sources of heat.

☐ Curtains and towels are kept away from stoves and portable heaters.

Fire Department

Write the telephone number of your fire department on this phone.

Fire Safety Code

To find out some things you should do in case of a fire, write the letter that stands for each symbol in the sentences below

A = ✚   B = ━   C = ✕   D = ☑   E = ⬇   F = ♤

G = ♣   H = ☐   I = ■   K = ⊠   L = ⬡   M = ⊘

N = ⊗   O = ✙   P = ♠   R = ☾   S = ◇   T = ●

U = ★   V = ☆   W = ≡   X = ⬡

1. If your ___ ___ ___ ___ ___ ___ ___ catch fire, ___ ___ ___ ___, ___ ___ ___ ___,
   and ___ ___ ___ ___.

2. Never ___ ___ ___ ___ ___ ___ into a ___ ___ ___ ___ ___ ___ ___
   ___ ___ ___ ___ ___ ___ ___ ___.

3. If you ___ ___ ___ ___ ___ ___ ___ ___ ___ ___, drop down and
   ___ ___ ___ ___ ___ ___ ___ ___ ___ ___ ___ ___.

4. Use ___ ___ ___ ___ ___ ___, never ___ ___ ___ ___ ___ ___ ___ ___ ___.

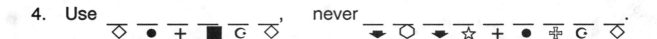

Name _____ Date _____

North to Alaska

(Alaska Day Festival, October 18)

Alaska was purchased from Russia in 1867, but it did not become a state until 1959. Although it is the largest state in the United States, it has the fewest people of any other state. Find out more about Alaska by labeling the following landmarks:

- Juneau (state capital)
- Mount McKinley (highest peak in the U.S.)
- Trans-Alaskan Pipeline
- Yukon River
- Arctic Ocean
- Pacific Ocean
- Canada

Potato Dishes

(Potetserie Day, October 28)

Potatoes grow all over the world. They are rich in vitamin C and contain many minerals including potassium and iron. In addition, they are very versatile and can be prepared in many different ways. Read the potato dishes and products on the potato. Then write them in alphabetical order on the lines below.

dumplings   whipped

salad

baked   french fries

mashed

boiled

pancakes   soup

scalloped

chips   skins

1. _____   7. _____

2. _____   8. _____

3. _____   9. _____

4. _____   10. _____

5. _____   11. _____

6. _____   12. _____

☆ Write the name of your favorite potato dish on the line below.

_____

Nevada Day

(Nevada Day, October 31)

Fill in the puzzle with words from the WORD BANK. Some clues are given to help you.

Fill in the blanks in the paragraph below with words from the WORD BANK.

On ① __ __ __ __ **b** __ __ 31, 1864 Nevada became the 36th

② __ __ __ __ **e** . Because

of the vast amounts of

③ __ __ __ **v** __ __ once mined there,

it is nicknamed the Silver State. The name

Nevada comes from a Spanish word which means

④ __ __ __ **w** — __ __ __ __ . The state flower is the

⑤ __ __ **g** __ __ __ __ __ and the state bird is the mountain

⑥ __ **l** __ __ __ __ __ __ . ⑦ __ __ __ __ **d** __ attracts about 30

million ⑧ __ __ **u** __ __ __ __ __ a year.

Carson City

Las Vegas

WORD   BANK

Nevada	October		bluebird	tourists
state	snow-clad		silver	sagebrush

Canada's Thanksgiving Day

(Second Monday in October)

We usually think that the Pilgrims started the tradition of Thanksgiving in the colony of Plymouth in 1621. However, 53 years before that the English settlers (under the leadership of Sir Martin Frobisher) held a harvest feast in Newfoundland, Canada. Today, the people of Canada celebrate Thanksgiving Day on the second Monday in October. Families and close friends gather to share dinner which includes turkey, mashed potatoes, cranberry sauce, and pumpkin pie.

To find out the names of two Canadian specialties which also may be served, answer the math problems below. Then place the letter that's next to your answer in the proper blank at the bottom of the page.

34
- 17
    =R
	48
	- 19
	    =S
		24
		+ 18
		    =I
			33
			- 14
			    =C

16
+ 25
    =A
	34
	- 26
	    =U
		29
		+ 16
		    =M
			17
			+ 15
			    =P

42
- 28
    =L
	45
	- 19
	    =E
		28
		+ 28
		    =Y
			21
			+ 19
			    =D

W __ __ __   __ __ __ __   and
  42 14 40   17 42 19 26

__ __ __ __ __   __ __ __ __ __   __ __ __ .
45 41 32 14 26   29 56 17 8 32   32 42 26

October Management

- Clip Art
- Contracts and Awards
- Holiday Report Form
- A Month of Dictionary Exercises
- And More!

Hot Tips!

Do you find yourself using the same method to get your students to line up for dismissals? Try this procedure instead. Make a set of number cards and pass them out randomly to the students. Then have them line up numerically. Another time, have them line up from the largest number to the smallest number.

Make fragrant awards! Sprinkle your awards with flavored extract (peppermint, banana, almond, etc.) or dry powdered drink mix.

Creative Writing

_____

_____

_____

_____

_____

_____

_____

_____

_____

_____

_____

_____

_____

_____

_____

_____

_____

_____

_____

_____

_____

A Month of Dictionary Exercises

In honor of Noah Webster, who was one of the first persons to write a dictionary, have students do these dictionary exercises. Supply each student or pair of students with a dictionary and assign a different activity each day throughout the month. At the end of each day's exercise, compare lists. Challenge students to find more than the assigned number of words.

1.	Write a list of ten words that end in -tion.	16.	Write a list of eight words that contain double l's.
2.	Write a list of eight words that end in the letter y.	17.	Write a list of ten words that end in -le.
3.	Write a list of six words that have four syllables.	18.	Write a list of eight words that have the accent on the second syllable.
4.	Write a list of ten words that contain two different vowels.	19.	Write a list of ten words that contain a "b" but do not begin with "b".
5.	Write a list of ten words that contain one pair of double consonants.	20.	Write a list of eight words that contain two vowels next to each other.
6.	Write a list of six words that end in -ite.	21.	Write a list of six words that contain an x and a y.
7.	Write a list of eight words that have two or more meanings.	22.	Write a list of twelve words that end in -ant.
8.	Write a list of twelve words that contain double vowels.	23.	Write a list of ten words that end in -es.
9.	Write a list of six words that have two spellings (theater, theatre).	24.	Write a list of ten words that end in -ank.
10.	Write a list of six words that are compound words.	25.	Write a list of twelve words that contain an "i" and a "t."
11.	Write a list of ten words that end in -king.	26.	Write a list of eight words that contain exactly eight letters.
12.	Write a list of eight words that end in -ize.	27.	Write a list of six words that have two different pronunciations.
13.	Write a list of ten words that begin or end in -ph.	28.	Write a list of eight words that end in -or.
14.	Write a list of six words that contain two r's.	29.	Write a list of six words that contain three different vowels.
15.	Write a list of eight words that have three syllables.	30.	Write a list of ten words that begin and end with the same letter.

Sense Matrix

(See page 23 for information)

Subject ___	Looks	Feels	Smells	Tastes	Sounds

Science Experiment Form

Name(s)_____

Title of Experiment_____

Question: What do we want to find out?

?

_____
_____
_____
_____
_____

Hypothesis: What do we think we will find out?

_____
_____
_____
_____
_____

Procedure: How will we find out?   (List step-by-step)

1. _____
   _____

2. _____
   _____
   _____

3. _____
   _____

4. _____
   _____

Results: What actually happened?

_____
_____
_____
_____

Conclusions: What did we learn?

_____
_____
_____
_____
_____

October Record Form

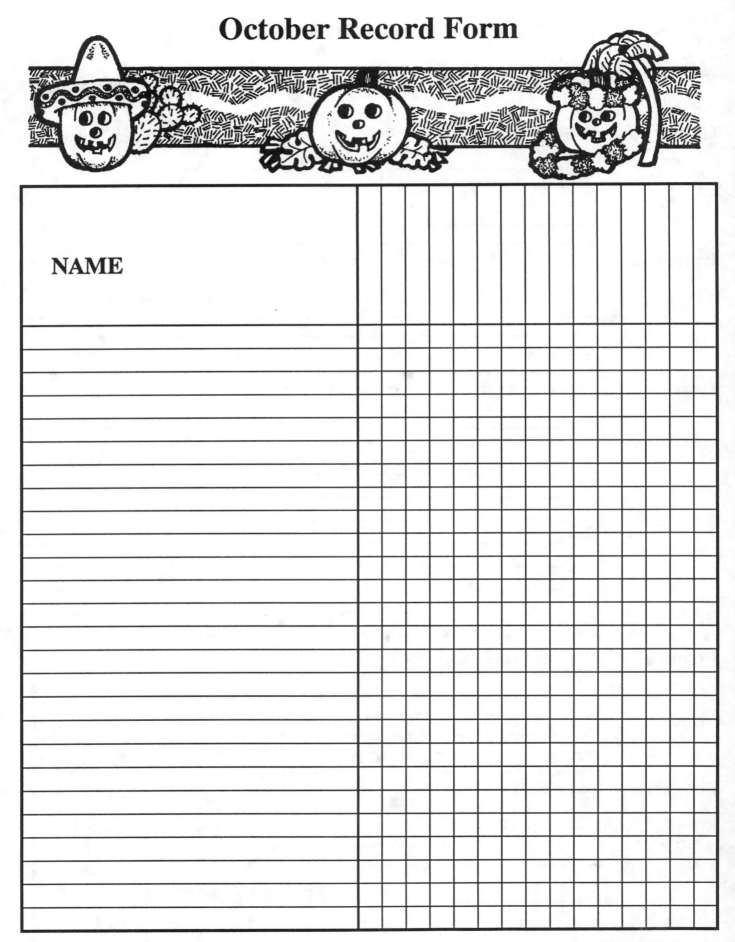

NAME												

Homework!

Write your assignments in the spaces below. Check them off as you complete them.

Reading

Mon. _____

Tues. _____

Wed. _____

Thurs. _____

Fri. _____

Language

Mon. _____

Tues. _____

Wed. _____

Thurs. _____

Fri. _____

Math

Mon. _____

Tues. _____

Wed. _____

Thurs. _____

Fri. _____

Science

Mon. _____

Tues. _____

Wed. _____

Thurs. _____

Fri. _____

Social Studies

Mon. _____

Tues. _____

Wed. _____

Thurs. _____

Fri. _____

Other

Mon. _____

Tues. _____

Wed. _____

Thurs. _____

Fri. _____

Thanks/Invitation

You're Invited

Thank You

Contract/Award

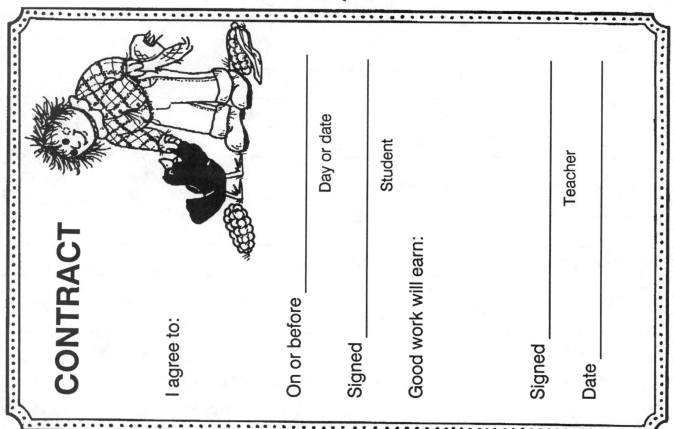

CONTRACT

I agree to:

On or before _____ Day or date

Signed _____ Student

Good work will earn:

Signed _____ Teacher

Date _____

AWARD

This is to certify that _____
Name

did **EXCELLENT WORK** in:

Congratulations!

_____
Teacher

_____
Date

We're Going on a Field Trip!

Where: _____

_____

When: _____

_____

Why: _____

_____

How: _____

_____

Please bring: _____

_____

_____

Please sign the permission slip below and have your child return it by _____

_____. Your child will not be allowed to go without the slip.

Thank you.

_____
Teacher

✂ -

My child, _____, has my permission to participate in the field trip

to _____.

_____
Parent

☐ I would like to chaperone. Please contact me!

56

Book Report Ideas

For a change of pace, assign one of the following projects instead of the standard written book report. Or, give students a choice of three out of five activities. Set aside enough time so students can share their ideas, and create a special area to display finished projects.

- *Compose a song or write a poem about the story. Recite your poem for the class; teach your song to your classmates.*

- *Build a diorama of the setting of the story or of one scene in the story that you especially enjoyed.*

- *Write a newspaper, magazine, radio, or television ad to attract others to read the book. Perform your ad with a friend for the group.*

- *Draw a map of the story's setting. Include important geographic features, such as lakes, rivers, etc. Explain the events that took place at various locations.*

- *Create a game related to the story. Make up your own rules and game cards. Teach other students how to play the game.*

- *Re-write the story in cartoon strip form. Create your own cartoon versions of characters and write their dialogue in bubbles. Share your completed cartoon with some younger children.*

- *Construct a time line to show the sequence of events in the story. Tape 8 1/2 x 11 inch sheets of paper together in a long row. Write and illustrate one event per page. Display your time line on a classroom wall.*

- *Make finger puppets depicting the characters. With a friend, act out some parts of the story.*

- *Create a poster to advertise the story so people will want to read it.*

- *Plan a meal for one of the characters of the story. Glue pictures to a paper plate of food items that you think the character would enjoy.*

Wanted!

Make a "Wanted!" poster for one of the characters in a book you have just read. Draw a picture of the character in the rectangle and write the character's name under the picture. Then fill in the blanks below.

WANTED!

Name: _____

Wanted for: _____

_____

_____

Looks: _____

_____

_____

Last seen: _____

_____

_____

Reward: _____

_____

_____

58

October Bookmarks

Materials

- *bookmark pattern*
- *tagboard*
- *crayons or colored markers*
- *scissors*

completed
project

Directions

Note: *Make a pattern out of tagboard. Have the child use the pattern to make his own bookmark.*

1. Trace around pattern onto tagboard.

2. Draw an object, animal, or other shape in the square at the top of the bookmark pattern. (Supply the spider, firefighter's hat, or ship patterns below, if desired.)

3. Cut out.

4. Color the design with crayons or marking pens.

bookmark
pattern

Have children record words they do not know from a particular reading selection on the bookmark's handle. In their free time they can look up the meaning of the words.

Name _____   Date _____

Holiday Report

Name of holiday: _____

Date it is celebrated: _____

Date it was first celebrated: _____

Historical events and people that led to its celebration:

_____

_____

_____

Type of holiday (circle answers):   local   state   national   religious

Draw some symbols of this holiday.	List some stories, poems, or songs associated with this holiday.
	_____ _____ _____ _____ _____ _____
This holiday's colors and what they mean. _____ _____ _____ _____ _____	Traditions, customs, or celebrations associated with this holiday. _____ _____ _____ _____ _____

Cloud Chart

How often do you notice cloud formations? October is a good month to observe clouds because of the many weather changes at this time of year. Use the pictures and descriptions below to chart the clouds for a month. Duplicate this page and cut out the pictures. Each day have students place the one that matches the weather that day on a classroom calendar.

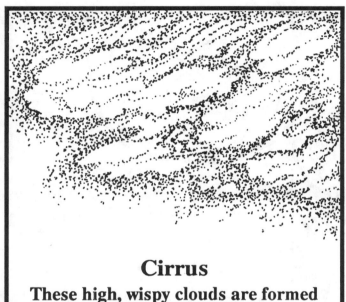

Cirrus
These high, wispy clouds are formed entirely of ice crystals.

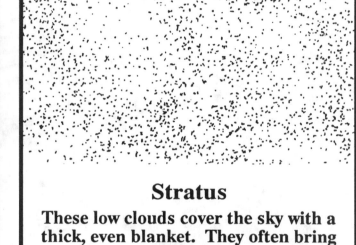

Stratus
These low clouds cover the sky with a thick, even blanket. They often bring rain or snow.

Cumulus
These heaped-up clouds rise up to great heights. They may bring rain, thunder, and lightning.

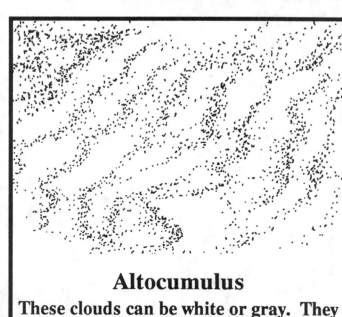

Altocumulus
These clouds can be white or gray. They form a sheet across the sky.

Clip Art

62

Big Patterns

Big Patterns
(cont.)

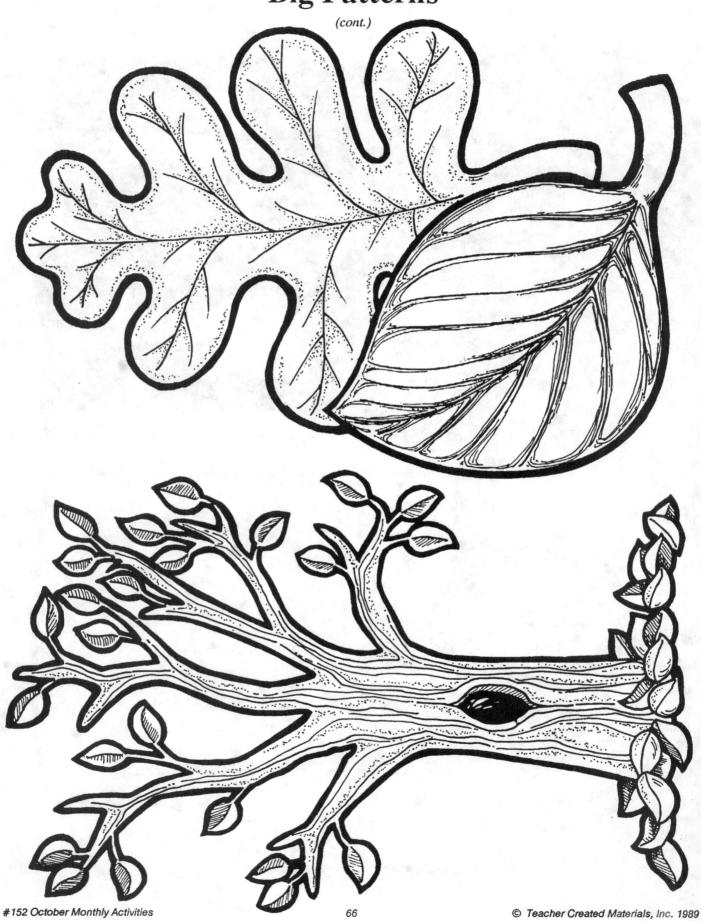

66

Big Patterns

(cont.)

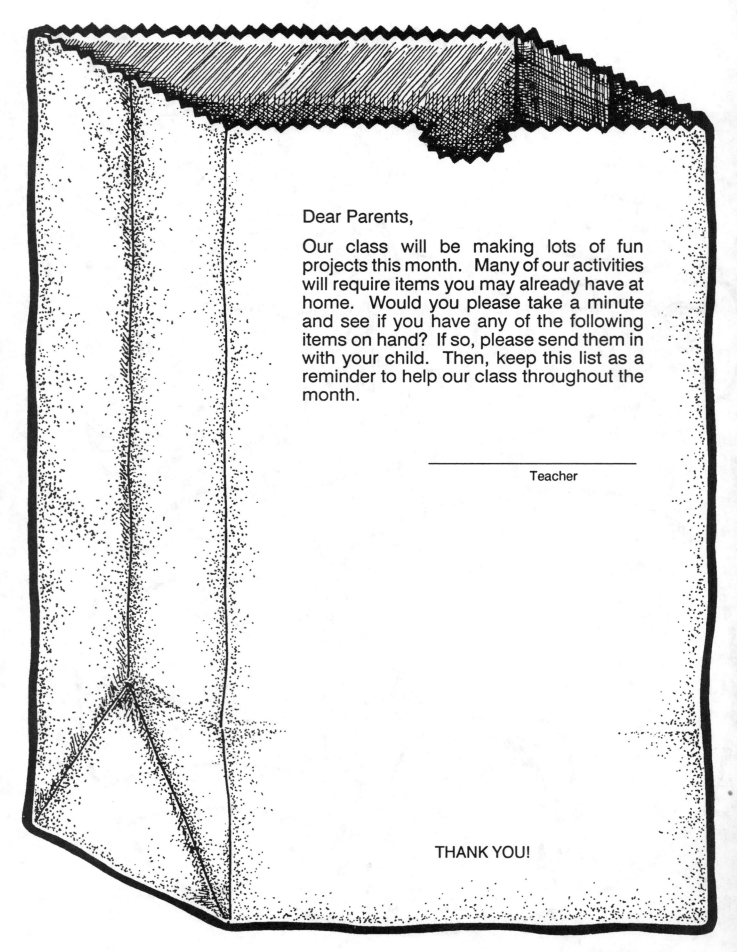

Dear Parents,

Our class will be making lots of fun projects this month. Many of our activities will require items you may already have at home. Would you please take a minute and see if you have any of the following items on hand? If so, please send them in with your child. Then, keep this list as a reminder to help our class throughout the month.

_____
Teacher

THANK YOU!

68

October
Bulletin Board

- Complete Directions
- Patterns
- Suggested Uses

Duplicate the patterns on orange construction paper. Have the students cut out yellow or black shapes to make facial features for their jack-o-lanterns.

Line the background of the bulletin board with felt. Glue sandpaper or nylon material strips (which can easily be pressed together and pulled apart) to the back of each pumpkin and leaf. Use them in a manipulative matching game.

Pumpkin Patch

OBJECTIVES

This interactive bulletin board can be used to teach or reinforce math, reading, social studies, and language skills. Some suggestions are given below.

MATERIALS

colored construction paper   thick green yarn   scissors

optional: felt, sandpaper   stapler   push pins

CONSTRUCTION

- Duplicate patterns onto appropriately colored construction paper and cut out.

- Assemble all pieces onto background; attach with staples or push pins. If using a felt background, glue sandpaper to the back of each piece and attach to bulletin board.

- With yarn, make a vine connecting the pumpkins, or draw one onto the background with chalk.

DIRECTIONS

- **Everyone Is Beautiful!** Assign each small group a different ethnic origin and have them create an "authentic" pumpkin for that ethnic group. You'll have a mini-United Nations bulletin board!

- **Work Bank.** With the class, brainstorm October words, pumpkin words or autumn words. Record words on the pumpkins for easy reference when doing creative writing assignments.

- **Matching.** Label each pumpkin with a different numeral. Label the leaves with different math facts. Students match all the different names for each number.

Hot Tip!

An easy way to group students for an art project is by passing out playing cards from an ordinary deck of cards. All the 3's are in one group, all the kings are in another group, etc.

Pumpkin Patch
(cont.)

Scarecrow

Attach bottom half of Scarecrow   (page 72) here.

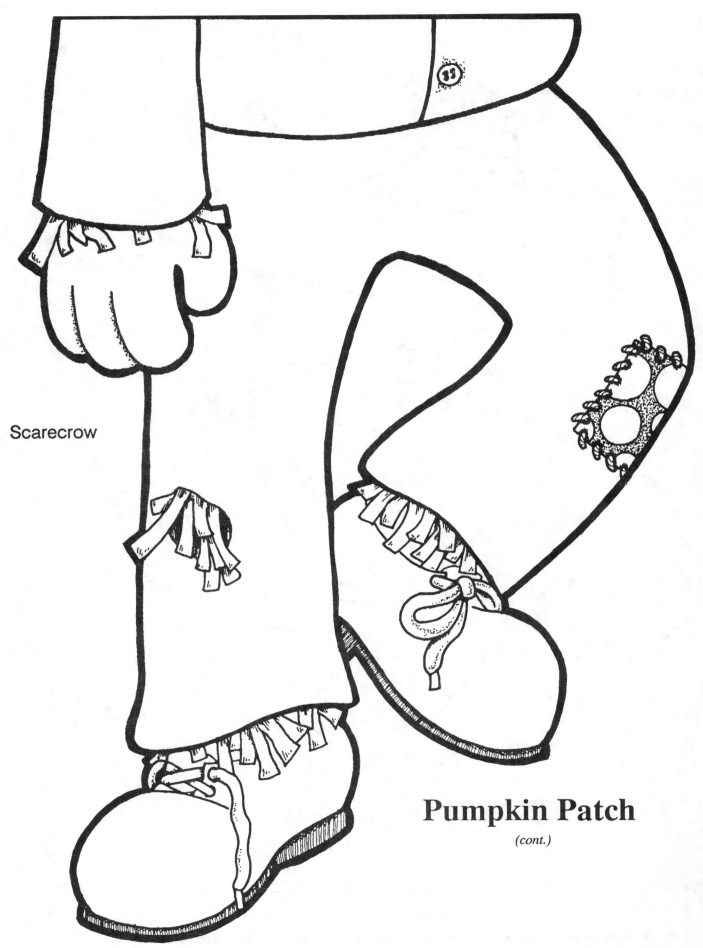

Scarecrow

Pumpkin Patch

(cont.)

72

Pumpkin Patch

(cont.)

Pumpkin Pattern

Make as many
as needed.

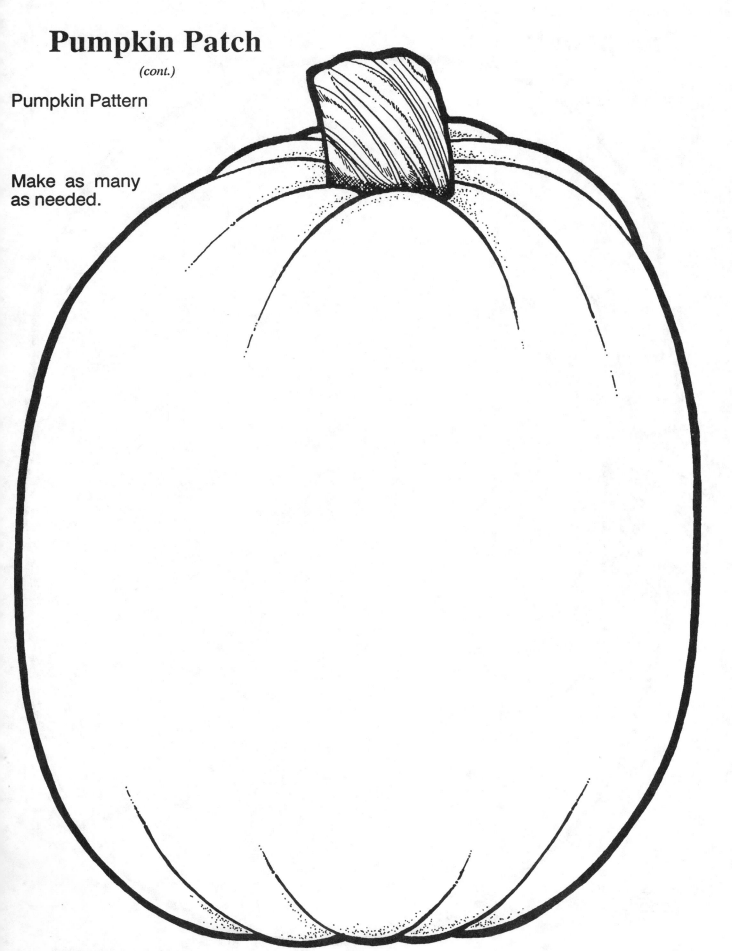

Pumpkin Patch
(cont.)

Pumpkin Pattern

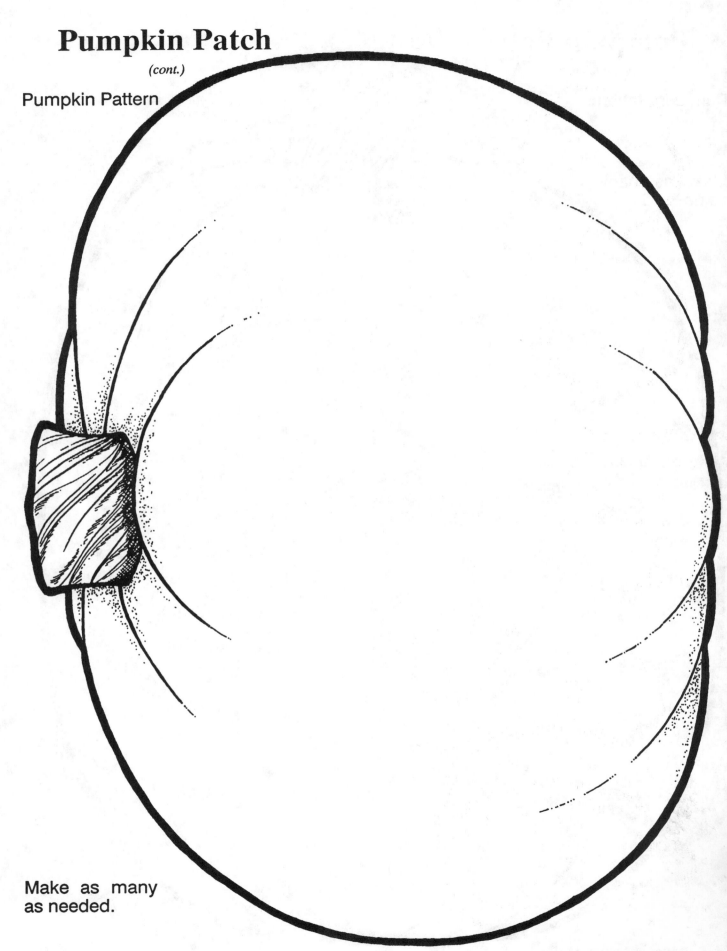

Make as many
as needed.

Pumpkin Patch

(cont.)

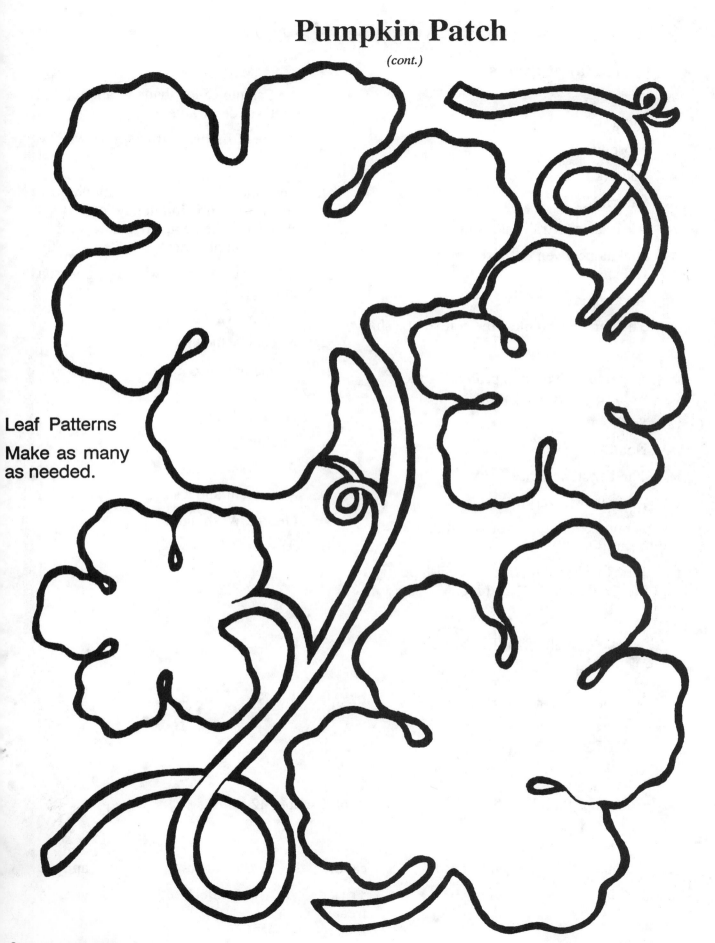

Leaf Patterns

Make as many
as needed.

Answer Key

p. 8-9 Calendar of Events

1. Africa
2. India
3. Mosquito
4. Sputnik I
5. Saturn V
6. Air brakes for railroad trains
7. Nickname given to those who reside in Indiana
8. An airplane pilot
9. The person who plots the course of a ship
10. Answers will vary.
11. A person devoted to promoting the welfare of people
12. Spain
13. Nautilus
14. The Keystone State
15. Answers will vary.
16. A book containing words and their definitions
17. First black in America to publish poetry. He lived from 1711 to 1790

18. An Eskimo canoe made of animal skins on a wooden frame
19. A type of firearm with a long barrel
20. 91
21. The Nobel Prize, an international prize given for distinction in physics, chemistry, medicine, literature, and promotion of peace
22. A heavy cloud mass with high peaks; a thundercloud
23. Answers will vary.
24. Answers will vary.
25. A type of ballroom dance done to 3/4 time
26. *The Jazz Singer*
27. The teddy bear
28. Answers will vary.
29. A crescent and a star
30. George Washington
31. Answers will vary.

p. 15

p. 34 Columbus found the New World, America, on October 12, 1492.

p. 35

1. October
2. holiday
3. children
4. ghosts
5. candy
6. Trick or treat
7. parties
8. cider
9. apples
10. game

Answer Key

(cont.)

p. 37

1. candy
2. mask
3. pumpkin
4. black
5. costume
6. orange
7. ghost
8. treat
9. spooky
10. apple

p. 40

1. aviator
2. poet
3. president
4. chef
5. scientist
6. composer
7. writer
8. inventor

p. 42

1. If your clothes catch fire, stop, drop, and roll.
2. Never go back into a burning building.
3. If you smell smoke, drop down and crawl to an exit.
4. Use stairs, never elevators.

p. 43   Alaska map

p. 44

1. baked
2. boiled
3. chips
4. dumplings
5. french fries
6. mashed
7. pancakes
8. salad
9. scalloped
10. skins
11. soup
12. whipped

p. 45

1. October
2. state
3. silver
4. snow-clad
5. sagebrush
6. bluebird
7. Nevada
8. tourists

p. 46   Wild rice and maple syrup pie

Open Worksheet Skills

These pages are ready to use. Simply fill in the directions and write the skill you want to reinforce. Make a copy for each student or pair of students or glue the worksheet to tagboard and laminate. Place at an appropriate classroom center; students can use water-based pens for easy wipe off and subsequent use. Ideas and resources for programming these worksheets are provided below and on the following pages.

Math

Basic Facts
Comparing numbers and fractions
Decimals
Word problems
Time
Place value
Skip counting
Ordinal numbers (1st, 2nd, 3rd, etc.)

Sets
Missing addends
Money problems
Geometric shapes
Measurement
Word names for numbers
Sequence
Percent

Roman Numerals

I - 1
II - 2
III - 3
IV - 4
V - 5

VI - 6
VII - 7
VIII - 8
IX - 9
X - 10

L - 50
C - 100
D - 500
M - 1,000
$\overline{\text{L}}$ - 50,000

Metric Measurement

mm - millimeter (1/10 cm)
cm - centimeter (10 mm)
dm - decimeter (10 cm)
m - meter (1,000 mm)
km - kilometer (1,000 m)

g - gram
kg - kilogram (1,000 g)
1 - liter (1,000 mL)
mL - milliliter
cc - cubic centimeter

Measurement Equivalents

12 in. = 1 ft.
3 ft. = 1 yd.
5,280 ft. = 1 mi.

4 qt. = 1 gal.
2 pt. = 1 qt.
8 oz. = 1 c.

1 t. = 2,000 lbs.
60 sec. = 1 min.
60 min, = 1 hr.

Open Worksheet Skills

(cont.)

Abbreviations

Names of states	dr. - drive	mt. - mountain
Days of the week	ave. - avenue	p. - page
Units of measurement	Dr. - Doctor	etc. - et cetera
Months of the year	Mrs. - Misses	yr. - year
blvd. - boulevard	Mr. - Mister	wk. - week
rd. - road	Gov. - Governor	
st. - street	Pres. - President	

Contractions

isn't - is not	I've - I have	they'd - they would
doesn't - does not	we've - we have	you'll - you will
haven't - have not	I'm - I am	won't - will not
hasn't - has not	you're - you are	I'm - I am
that's - that is	it's - it is	let's - let us

Compound Words

airplane	bodyguard	everywhere	percent
anyhow	bookcase	footnote	quarterback
anything	cardboard	grandfather	snowflake
basketball	classroom	handwriting	suitcase
bedroom	earthquake	makeup	watermelon

Prefixes

dis -	**un -**	**over -**	**re -**
disapprove	uncut	overcharge	recover
discolor	uneven	overdressed	redo
discount	unfair	overdue	reheat
dislike	unhappy	overfeed	remiss
dismay	unlike	overgrown	replay
dismiss	unmade	overpaid	reset
disobey	unwashed	overrun	review

Suffixes

- ful	**- less**	**- ly**	**- en**
beautiful	ageless	actively	harden
careful	homeless	happily	moisten
helpful	priceless	quickly	sweeten
skillful	worthless	silently	thicken

Open Worksheet Skills

(cont.)

Plurals

- s

toe	kitten
pin	window
lamp	star
book	key

- es

church	class
lunch	inch
box	tomato
brush	waltz

- ies

sky	cherry
baby	body
party	army
family	lady

Anagrams

dear - dare - read
notes - stone - tones
fowl - flow - wolf
veil - vile - evil - live
tea - ate - eat

shoe - hoes - hose
vase - save
pea - ape
north - thorn
flea - leaf

veto - vote
cone - once
stop - tops - pots - post - spot
steam - meats - mates - tames

Synonyms

sleepy - tired
firm - solid
story - tale
shut - close
easy - simple

wealthy - rich
quick - fast
sea - ocean
icy - cold
chore - task

friend - pal
tiny - small
jump - leap
gift - present
hike - walk

Antonyms

empty - full
tame - wild
city - country
faster - slower
strong - weak

tall - short
rough - smooth
light - dark
dirty - clean
calm - nervous

correct - wrong
forget - remember
thick - slender
sweet - sour
young - aged

Homonyms

eight - ate
whole - hole
red - read
hour - our
peace - piece

lone - loan
pale - pail
knew - new
nose - knows
blew - blue

would - wood
for - four - fore
by - buy - bye
sense - cents - scents
two - too - to